Ring Bearer A to Z

Penelope Colville Paine

Paper Posie

For Carson Henry Bennett and Clay Henderson Bennett

Paper Posie

Published by Paper Posie, Santa Barbara, CA
(800) 360-1761

Copyright © 2009 Penelope C. Paine
ISBN: 978-0-9774763-4-3

To see all Paper Posie's products for children at weddings visit:
www.paperposie.com

Editor: Gail M. Kearns, www.topressandbeyond.com

Production: Cathy Feldman

Design and Typography: Peri Poloni-Gabriel, Knockout Design
www.knockoutbooks.com

Photography includes work by:
Dia Rao Photography — www.diaraophotography.com
Charles Harvey Bennett

Special thanks to Charles and Diane, Carson and Clay Bennett

1 2 3 4 5 6 7 8 9 10

Printed in China

This Book
Belongs To:

_____

The Bride and
Groom Are:

_____

_____

Wedding Date:

_____

_____

B is for your *Boutonniere*, the *Bride* and *Balloons*

C is for Cake and Candy so sweet

$\mathcal{D}$ is for a great Day for families to meet

E is for Exciting and having lots of fun

F is for Favors given out to everyone

G is for the Groom,

and a Gift just for you

H is for Helping him

as ring bearers do

I is for Invitations sent out in the mail

J is for Jewels in the bride's ring and her veil

K is for Kisses and hugs, so please don't hide!

L is for Limousine and a super smooth ride

M is for Music, you'll love to dance to the beat

N is for Nighttime and staying up late for a treat

O is for *Oh,* how handsome you look

P is for Photos to keep in a book

Q is for quiet

while the ceremony takes place

R is for the Ring Pillow and Rings tied with lace

S is for Shiny new Shoes and your Smile

T is for Tuxedo and a Bow Tie, what style!

U is for ushers who welcome guests with great care

V is for *Vows* that the bride and groom will share

W is for Wedding Bells that ring out to say

X is for X-TRA cool and an extra great day

Y is for YOU, the best ring bearer I know

Z is for ZZZs, your sleepy head on a pillow

Hope you enjoy being a Ring Bearer...